Early praise for *Exercises for Programmers*

If you're looking to pick up a new programming language, you should also pick up this book. You'll learn how to solve problems from first principles, developing a stronger foundation to build on top of. I learned a lot. I expect you will too.

➤ **Stephen Orr**
Senior software engineer, Impact Applications

A wonderful resource for learning new languages using the most effective method: practice. Because the book is language agnostic, it has almost endless replay value, which is a rare quality among technical books.

➤ **Jason Pike**
Software developer, theswiftlearner.com

This is a wonderful book for anyone who wants to start fresh in a new language. Programmers new and old will greatly benefit from this repository of exercises. This book offers comfort for beginners and challenges for advanced programmers.

➤ **Alex Henry**
Software engineer quality assurance, JAMF Software

Exercises for Programmers

57 Challenges to Develop Your Coding Skills

Brian P. Hogan

The Pragmatic Bookshelf

Dallas, Texas • Raleigh, North Carolina

Many of the designations used by manufacturers and sellers to distinguish their products are claimed as trademarks. Where those designations appear in this book, and The Pragmatic Programmers, LLC was aware of a trademark claim, the designations have been printed in initial capital letters or in all capitals. The Pragmatic Starter Kit, The Pragmatic Programmer, Pragmatic Programming, Pragmatic Bookshelf, PragProg and the linking *g* device are trademarks of The Pragmatic Programmers, LLC.

Every precaution was taken in the preparation of this book. However, the publisher assumes no responsibility for errors or omissions, or for damages that may result from the use of information (including program listings) contained herein.

Our Pragmatic courses, workshops, and other products can help you and your team create better software and have more fun. For more information, as well as the latest Pragmatic titles, please visit us at *https://pragprog.com*.

The team that produced this book includes:

Susannah Davidson Pfalzer (editor)
Linda Recktenwald (copyedit)
Dave Thomas (layout)
Janet Furlow (producer)
Ellie Callahan (support)

For international rights, please contact *rights@pragprog.com*.

Printed in the United States of America.
ISBN-13: 978-1-68050-122-3
Printed on acid-free paper.
Book version: P1.0—September 2015

Contents

Acknowledgments

First, thank you. You're awesome. No, you really are, because you've picked up this book and made a commitment to improving your skills as a software developer. I wrote this book for people just like you, so thank you for reading.

Second, thank you, Dave Thomas, for believing in this idea and for your guidance over the years. It's been an honor and a privilege to learn from you. Your encouragement on this book means a lot, and I appreciate your generosity with your time as you reviewed the exercises and offered suggestions. You and Andy continue to make the world better for programmers, and I'm grateful to be able to contribute to that in my small way.

A special thank you to Susannah Pfalzer. You always make my books better than they started out. You seem to catch all the right details, and you guide me to focus on what really matters. This is the sixth book you've helped me with, and I'm a better writer because of all your guidance over the years.

Next, thank you, Andy Hunt, Mike Reilly, Michael Swaine, Fahmida Rashid, and Bruce Tate, for your encouragement when I proposed this idea.

The programs in this book are ones I've been using to teach programming over the last ten years. Thank you to Zachary Baxter, Jordan Berg, Luke Chase, Dee Dee Dale, Jacob Donahoe, Alex Eckblad, Arrio Farugie, Emily Mikl, Aaron Miller, Eric Mohr, Zachary Solofra, Darren Sopiarz, Ashley Stevens, Miah Thalacker, Andrew Walley, and all the other students who've come through my classes and training sessions over the years. The feedback you've provided on my approach to teaching has helped me immensely. And thank you, Kyle

Loewenhagen, Jon Cooley, and George Andrews, for helping me grow as a teacher with your feedback and insights.

Thank you, Deb Walsh, for your encouragement and incredible ideas on how to get the best out of students. We share core beliefs about teaching and learning, and I learn so much from our conversations. Thank you for sharing your experience and expertise with me and for your support of my teaching methods.

This book of exercises flows much better and is clarified by the fantastic feedback from a great mix of new and veteran software developers. Each reviewer put an incredible amount of time and effort into working through these problems in their favorite programming language, helping me identify things that didn't make sense or needed improvement. Thank you, Chris C., Alex Henry, Jessica Janiuk, Chris Johnson, Aaron Kalair, Sean Lindsay, Matthew Oldham, Stephen Orr, Jason Pike, Jessica Stodola, Andrew Vahey, and Mitchell Volk, for donating your valuable time to test these exercises and provide suggestions and feedback.

Thank you to my business associates Mitch Bullard, Kevin Gisi, Chris Johnson, Jeff Holland, Erich Tesky, Myles Steinhauser, Chris Warren, and Mike Weber for your support.

Thank you, Carissa, my wonderful wife and best friend. Your love and support make this all possible. I am forever grateful for all you do for me and our girls.

Finally, thank you, Ana, for being awesome, and thank you, Lisa, for all the hugs and text messages while I was writing. And for keeping me company on the couch while I wrote this.

How to Use This Book

Practice makes permanent.

A concert pianist practices many hours a day, learning music, practicing drills, and honing her skills. She practices the same piece of music over and over, learning every little detail to get it just right. Because when she performs, she wants to deliver a performance she is proud of for the people who spent their time and money to hear it.

A pro football player spends hours in the gym lifting, running, jumping, and doing drills over and over until he masters them. And then he practices the sport. He'll study plays and watch old game videos. And, of course, he'll play scrimmage and exhibition games to make sure he's ready to perform during the real contest.

A practitioner of karate spends a lifetime doing *kata,* a series of movements that imitate a fight or battle sequence, learning how to breathe and flex the right muscles at the right time. She may do the same series of movements thousands of times, getting better and better with each repetition.

The best software developers I've ever met approach their craft the same way. They don't go to work every day and practice on the employer's dime. They invest personal time in learning new languages and perfecting techniques in others. Of course they learn new things on the job, but because they're getting paid, there's an expectation that they are there to perform, not practice.

This book is all about practicing your craft as a programmer. Flip to a page in this book, crack open your text editor, and hammer out the program. Make your own variations on it.

Do it in a language you've never used before. And get better and better each time you do it.

Who This Book Is For

This book is targeted at two main groups of programmers.

First, it's for beginning programming students to get additional practice beyond the classroom. You can't hone your skills just by doing your assignments. Your future employer will want you to be able to demonstrate critical thinking and problem-solving skills, and you need practice to develop those. This book gives you that practice in the form of real-world problems that many developers face but that are geared toward your abilities. Each chapter covers a fundamental component of programming and is a little more complex than the previous one, building on what you've learned and preparing you for the challenges that lie ahead, both in and out of the classroom.

Many beginning programmers are used to being told exactly how to solve a problem. They often learn a language by following a written tutorial that has some code they can type. And this is a great way to start writing code. But these programmers struggle when faced with open-ended problems that don't have the solution available. And as anyone who has experience can tell you, software development is full of open-ended problems. The exercises in this book help you develop those problem-solving skills so that you build the confidence to attack even larger problems—maybe even ones that nobody else has solved yet.

But this book is also for experienced programmers looking to get better at what they do. When I learned Go and Elixir, I used programs like the ones in this book. When I tried my hand at iOS development, I tried to write these programs. And every once in a while, I do these programs in a language I already know. I'm fluent in JavaScript and Ruby, and it's a great challenge to see if I can tackle one of these programs in a different way, using a different algorithm or pattern. When I started teaching Ruby and JavaScript full time, these programs helped me discover and explain the unique features of the languages I knew how to use but didn't quite fully understand. And so if you're an experienced developer, I encourage you to do the same. Try one of these programs in Haskell. Or try to write one of these programs in every language you know and compare the results. Challenge your coworkers to do one of these exercises a week and compare your solutions. Or use these programs to mentor the new junior developer on your team.

A Note for Educators

If you teach introductory programming at the high school or college level, you may find the exercises in this book useful in your class. I don't recommend using these as summative assessments though; people reading this book are encouraged to share their solutions with others. But I do recommend using these as in-class exercises where students can work together. These exercises work well in a problem-based learning environment.

What's in This Book (And What's Not)

This book is written first and foremost to provide beginners with challenging problems they might face when first learning to program. Therefore, most of the problems are relatively simple in the beginning and gradually get more complex. The progression of exercises in this book makes practicing the fundamentals of programming challenging but fun and can accelerate the process of picking up a new language. In the first section, the programs simply take some input and manipulate the data into different output, giving you experience with how computer programs handle input and output operations. They're the kind of programs you'd do in your first week as a beginning programmer.

Next, you'll be challenged by writing programs that have you do calculations. Some of them are as simple as calculating the area of a room. But others involve financial and medical calculations similar to ones you may find on the job.

Then you'll increase the complexity of your programs by including decision logic and repetition logic, and you'll incorporate functions into them.

After that you'll find some problems that need to be solved using data structures like arrays and maps. These programs also require you to draw on some of the other problems you've solved before.

And, of course, no collection of programs would be complete without a bit of file input and output, so you'll get to practice reading data from files, processing it, and writing it back out.

Modern programs often talk with external services, so you'll find a few programs that have you work with data using third-party APIs.

Finally, a few larger programs at the end will require you to put together all the things you've learned.

In addition, each exercise includes some constraints that you'll have to follow when building the program as well as some challenges that ask you to build on the program. If you've never programmed before, you may want to skip the challenges and revisit them when you improve your skills. But if you've got some experience under your belt, you may want to accept these challenges right away if you think the program is too simple. Some of the challenges will be difficult depending on the programming language you've chosen. For example, if you're creating these programs with JavaScript and HTML, making a GUI version of the program will be easy. If you're doing this with Java, it will be a lot more work. So feel free to modify the challenges as you see fit.

However, what you *won't* find in this book are the solutions to the programs. If you think hard enough and use all of the resources at your disposal, you'll be able to figure out how to solve these problems on your own, which is the point of this book.

One last thing: you won't find the infamous interview questions here. There's no FizzBuzz. You won't need to invert binary trees, nor will you need to write a quicksort algorithm (unless you want to as part of a solution). If you're looking for things like that, you'll have to look elsewhere. Those kinds of problems have value but are often more difficult to do because it's not clear why you're doing them. That makes them unapproachable, which creates a barrier to learning.

The problems in this book are simple, real-world problems that you can easily relate to and that will help you practice solving problems with code.

What You Need

All you need is your favorite development environment—or even one you've never used. This book is programming-language agnostic. Pick a language, grab that language's reference guide, and dive in. Be warned though; the programming language you choose will determine how easy, or difficult, these programs are. For example, if you choose to do this book with Python or Ruby, then developing graphical user interfaces won't be easy. And if you choose to use JavaScript in the browser, then working with external files and web services will be much more complex than with other languages. Your approach to problems will be much different if you choose a functional programming language over an object-oriented one. But that's the real value of these exercises; they'll help you learn a language *and how that language is different from what you already know.*

You should have an Internet connection so you can do some of the programs that use third-party services and participate in the community for this book.

Online Resources

The book's website [1] has a discussion forum where you can discuss the book with other developers. Feel free to post solutions there in your favorite language and discuss your solutions with other readers. One of the most fascinating things about programming is how people approach solving problems differently and how each developer has his or her own style.

---

1. http://pragprog.com/titles/bhwb

CHAPTER 1

Turning Problems into Code

If you're new to programming, you may wonder how experienced developers can look at a problem and turn it into runnable code. It turns out that writing the actual code is only a small part of the process. You have to break down the problem before you can solve it. If you've ever watched an experienced programmer, it may look like they just cracked open their code editor and banged out a solution. But over the years, they've broken down hundreds, if not thousands, of problems, and they can see patterns. If you're just starting out, you might not know how to do that. So in this chapter we'll look at one way to break down problems and turn them into code. And you can use this approach to conquer the problems in the rest of this book.

Understanding the Problem

One of the best ways to figure out what you have to do is to write it down. If I told you that I wanted a tip calculator application, would that be enough information for you to just go and build one? Probably not. You'd probably have to ask me a few questions. This is often called gathering requirements, but I like to think of it as figuring out what features the program should have.

Think of a few questions you could ask me that would let you get a clearer picture of what I want. What do you need to know to build this application?

Got some questions? Great. Here are some you might ask:

- What formula do you want to use? Can you explain how the tip should be calculated?
- What's the tip percentage? Is it 15% or should the user be able to modify it?
- What should the program display on the screen when it starts?
- What should the program display for its output? Do you want to see the tip and the total or just the total?

Once you have the answers to your questions, try writing out a problem statement that explains exactly what you're building. Here's the problem statement for the program we're going to build:

> Create a simple tip calculator. The program should prompt for a bill amount and a tip rate. The program must compute the tip and then display both the tip and the total amount of the bill.

Example output:

```
What is the bill? $200
What is the tip percentage? 15
The tip is $30.00
The total is $230.00
```

Joe asks:

What do I do with complex programs?

Break down the large program into smaller features that are easier to manage. If you do that, you'll have a better chance of success because each feature can be fleshed out. And most complex applications out there are composed of many smaller programs working together. That's how command-line tools in Linux work; one program's output can be another program's input.

If you're ready to open your text editor and hammer out the code, you're jumping way ahead of yourself. You see, if you don't take the time to carefully design the program, you might end up with something that works but isn't good quality. And unfortunately, it's very easy for something like that to get out into the wild. For example, you hammer out your program without testing, planning, or documenting it, and your boss sees it, thinks it's done, and tells you to release it. Now you have untested, unplanned code in production, and you'll probably be asked to make changes to it later. Code that's poorly designed is very hard to maintain or extend. So let's take this tip calculator example and go through a simple process that will help you understand what you're supposed to build.

Discovering Inputs, Processes, and Outputs

Every program has inputs, processes, and outputs, whether it's a simple program like this one or a complex application like Facebook. In fact, large applications are simply a bunch of smaller programs that communicate. The output of one program becomes the input of another.

You can ensure that both small and large programs work well if you take the time to clearly state what these inputs, processes, and outputs are. An easy way to do that, if you have a clear problem statement, is to look at the nouns and verbs in that statement. The nouns end up becoming your inputs and outputs, and the verbs will be your processes. Look at the problem statement for our tip calculator:

> Create a simple tip calculator. The program should prompt for a bill amount and a tip rate. The program must compute the tip and then display both the tip and the total amount of the bill.

First, look for the nouns. Circle them if you like, or just make a list. Here's my list:

- bill amount
- tip rate
- tip
- total amount

Now, what about the verbs?

- prompt
- compute
- display

So we know we have to prompt for inputs, do some calculations, and display some outputs. By looking at the nouns and verbs, we can get an idea of what we're being asked to do.

Of course, the problem statement won't always be clear. For example, the problem statement says we need to calculate the tip, but it then says we need to display the tip and the total. It's implied that we'll need to also add the tip to the original bill amount to get that output. And that's one of the challenges of building software. It isn't spelled out to you 100% of the time. But as you gain more experience, you'll be able to fill in the gaps and read between the lines.

So with a little bit of sleuthing, we determine that our inputs, processes, and outputs for this program look like this:

- Inputs: bill amount, tip rate
- Processes: calculate the tip
- Outputs: tip amount, total amount

Are we ready to start producing some code? Not just yet.

Driving Design with Tests

One of the best ways to design and develop software is to think about the result you want to get right from the start. Many professional software developers do this using a formal process called *test-driven development*, or *TDD*. In TDD, you write bits of code that test the outputs of your program or the outputs of the individual programs that make up a larger program. This process of testing as you go guides you toward good design and helps you think about the issues your program might have.

TDD does require some knowledge about the language you're using and a little more experience than the beginning developer has out of the gate.

However, the essence of TDD is to think about what the expected result of the program is ahead of time and then work toward getting there. And if you do that before you write code, it'll make you think beyond what the initial requirements say. So if you're not quite comfortable doing formal TDD, you can still get many of the benefits by creating simple test plans. A test plan lists the program's inputs and its expected result.

Here's what a test plan looks like:

```
Inputs:
Expected result:
Actual result:
```

You list the program inputs and then write out what the program's output should be. And then you run your program and compare the expected result with the actual result your program gives out.

Let's put this into practice by thinking about our tip calculator. How will we know what the program's output should be? How will we know if we calculate it correctly?

Well, let's *define* how we want things to work by using some test plans. We'll do a very simple test plan first.

```
Inputs:
  bill amount: 10
  tip rate: 15
Expected result:
  Tip: $1.50
  Total: $11.50
```

That test plan tells us a couple things. First, it tells us that we'll take in two inputs: a bill amount of 10 and a tip rate of 15. So we'll need to handle converting the tip rate from a whole number to a decimal when we do the math. It also tells us we'll print out the tip and total formatted as currency. So we know that we'd better do some conversions in our program.

Now, one test isn't enough. What if we used 11.25 as an input? Using a test plan, what should the output be? Try it out. Fill in the following plan:

```
Input:
  bill amount: 11.25
  tip rate: 15
Expected result:
  Tip: ???
  Total: ???
```

I assume you just went and used a calculator to figure out the tip. If you ran the calculation, your calculator probably said the tip should be 1.6875.

But is that realistic? Probably not. We would probably round up to the nearest cent. So our test plan would look like this:

```
Input:
  bill amount: 11.25
  tip rate: 15
Expected result:
  Tip: $1.69
  Total: $12.94
```

We just used a test to design the functionality of our program; we determined that our program will need to round up the answer.

When you're going through the exercises in this book, take the time to develop at least four test plans for every program, and try to think of as many scenarios as you can for how people might break the program. And as you get into the more complicated problems, you may need a lot more test plans.

If you're an experienced software developer who wants to get started with TDD, you should use the exercises in this book to get acquainted with the libraries and tools your favorite language has to offer. You can find a list of testing frameworks for many programming languages at Wikipedia.[1] You can read Kent Beck's *Test-Driven Development: By Example* to gain more insight into how to design code with tests, or you can investigate any number of more language-specific resources on TDD.

So now that we have a clearer picture of the features the program will have, we can start putting together the *algorithm* for the program.

Writing the Algorithm in Pseudocode

An algorithm is a step-by-step set of operations that need to be performed. If you take an algorithm and write code to

1. https://en.wikipedia.org/wiki/List_of_unit_testing_frameworks

perform those operations, you end up with a computer program.

If you're new to programming and not entirely comfortable with a programming language's syntax yet, you should consider writing out the algorithm using *pseudocode,* an English-like syntax that lets you think about the logic without having to worry about paper. Pseudocode isn't just for beginners; experienced programmers will occasionally write some pseudocode on a whiteboard when working with teammates to solve problems, or even by themselves.

There's no "right way" to write pseudocode, although there are some widely used terms. You might use Initialize to state that you're setting an initial value, Prompt to say that you're prompting for input, and Display to indicate what you're displaying on the screen.

Here's how our tip calculator might look in pseudocode:

```
TipCalculator
  Initialize billAmount to 0
  Initialize tip to 0
  Initialize tipRate to 0
  Initialize total to 0

  Prompt for billAmount with "What is the bill amount?"
  Prompt for tipRate with "What is the tip rate?"

  convert billAmount to a number
  convert tipRate to a number

  tip = billAmount * (tipRate / 100)
  round tip up to nearest cent
  total = billAmount + tip

  Display "Tip: $" + tip
  Display "Total: $" + total
End
```

That's a rough stab at how our program's algorithm will look. We'll have to set up some variables, make some decisions based on the input, do some conversions, and put some output on the screen. I recommend including details like variable names and text you'll display on the screen in pseudocode, because it helps you think more clearly about the end result of the program.

Is this the best way we could write the program? Probably not. But that's not the point. By writing pseudocode, we've created something we can show to another developer to get feedback, and it didn't take long to throw it together.

Best of all, we can use this as a blueprint to code this up in any programming language. Notice that our pseudocode makes no assumptions about the language we might end up using, but it does guide us as to what the variable names will be and what the output to the end user will look like.

Once you write your initial version of the program and get it working, you can start tweaking your code to improve it. For example, you may split the program into functions, or you may do the numerical conversions inline instead of as separate steps. Just think of pseudocode as a planning tool.

Writing the Code

Now it's your turn. Using what you've learned, can you write the code for this program? Give it a try. Just keep these constraints in mind as you do so:

Constraints

- Enter the tip as a percentage. For example, a 15% tip would be entered as 15, not 0.15. Your program should handle the division.
- Round fractions of a cent up to the next cent.

If you can't figure out how to enforce these constraints, write the program without them and come back to it later. The point of these exercises is to practice and improve.

And if this program is too challenging for you right now, jump ahead and do some of the easier programs in this book first, and then come back to this one.

Challenges

When you've finished writing the basic version of the program, try tackling some additional challenges:

- Ensure that the user can enter only numbers for the bill amount and the tip rate. If the user enters non-numeric values, display an appropriate message and exit the program. Here's a test plan as an example:

```
Input:
  bill amount: abcd
  tip rate: 15
Expected result: Please enter a valid number for
                 the bill amount.
```

- Instead of displaying an error message and exiting the program, keep asking the user for correct input until it is provided.
- Don't allow the user to enter a negative number.
- Break the program into functions that do the computations.
- Implement this program as a GUI program that automatically updates the values when any value changes.
- Instead of the user entering the value of the tip as a percentage, have the user drag a slider that rates satisfaction with the server, using a range between 5% and 20%.

Onward!

Try to tackle each problem in the book using this strategy to get the most out of the experience. Discover your inputs, processes, and outputs. Develop some test plans, come up with some pseudocode, and write the program. Then accept the various challenges after each program. Or go in your own direction. Or write the program in as many languages as you can.

But most of all, have fun and enjoy learning.

CHAPTER 2

Input, Processing, and Output

Getting input from the user and converting it to something meaningful is one of the fundamental pieces of programming. Software developers are always turning data into information that can be used to make decisions. That data may come from the keyboard, a mouse, a touch, a swipe, or even a game controller. The computer has to react to it, process it, and do something useful.

The exercises in this chapter will help you get acquainted with how to get input from the user and process it to produce output. You'll build up strings, do a little math, and get your feet wet with the programming language you're using. They're simple problems, but they'll help you build up your confidence as a programmer; the problems in the later chapters of the book are more complex.

Each exercise has additional challenges you can do if you feel up to the task. If you're new to programming, some of the challenges will ask you to use techniques you might not be familiar with yet. Feel free to skip them; you can always come back and do those challenges later.

Ready? Set? Go!

1 Saying Hello

The "Hello, World" program is the first program you learn to write in many languages, but it doesn't involve any input.

So create a program that prompts for your name and prints a greeting using your name.

Example Output

```
What is your name? Brian
Hello, Brian, nice to meet you!
```

Constraint

- Keep the input, string concatenation, and output separate.

Challenges

- Write a new version of the program without using any variables.
- Write a version of the program that displays different greetings for different people. This would be a good challenge to try after you've completed the exercises in Chapter 4, *Making Decisions*, on page 29 and Chapter 7, *Data Structures*, on page 63.

2 Counting the Number of Characters

Create a program that prompts for an input string and displays output that shows the input string and the number of characters the string contains.

Example Output

```
What is the input string? Homer
Homer has 5 characters.
```

Constraints

- Be sure the output contains the original string.
- Use a single output statement to construct the output.
- Use a built-in function of the programming language to determine the length of the string.

Challenges

- If the user enters nothing, state that the user must enter something into the program.
- Implement this program using a graphical user interface and update the character counter every time a key is pressed. If your language doesn't have a particularly friendly GUI library, try doing this exercise with HTML and JavaScript instead.

3 Printing Quotes

Quotation marks are often used to denote the start and end of a string. But sometimes we need to print out the quotation marks themselves by using *escape characters*.

Create a program that prompts for a quote and an author. Display the quotation and author as shown in the example output.

Example Output

```
What is the quote? These aren't the droids you're looking for.
Who said it? Obi-Wan Kenobi
Obi-Wan Kenobi says, "These aren't the droids
you're looking for."
```

Constraints

- Use a single output statement to produce this output, using appropriate string-escaping techniques for quotes.
- If your language supports string interpolation or string substitution, don't use it for this exercise. Use string concatenation instead.

Challenge

- In Chapter 7, *Data Structures*, on page 63, you'll practice working with lists of data. Modify this program so that instead of prompting for quotes from the user, you create a structure that holds quotes and their associated attributions and then display all of the quotes using the format in the example. An array of maps would be a good choice.

4 Mad Lib

Mad libs are a simple game where you create a story template with blanks for words. You, or another player, then construct a list of words and place them into the story, creating an often silly or funny story as a result.

Create a simple mad-lib program that prompts for a noun, a verb, an adverb, and an adjective and injects those into a story that you create.

Example Output

```
Enter a noun: dog
Enter a verb: walk
Enter an adjective: blue
Enter an adverb: quickly
Do you walk your blue dog quickly? That's hilarious!
```

Constraints

- Use a single output statement for this program.
- If your language supports string interpolation or string substitution, use it to build up the output.

Challenges

- Add more inputs to the program to expand the story.
- Implement a branching story, where the answers to questions determine how the story is constructed. You'll explore this concept more in the problems in Chapter 4, *Making Decisions*, on page 29.

5 Simple Math

You'll often write programs that deal with numbers. And depending on the programming language you use, you'll have to convert the inputs you get to numerical data types.

Write a program that prompts for two numbers. Print the sum, difference, product, and quotient of those numbers as shown in the example output:

Example Output

```
What is the first number? 10
What is the second number? 5
10 + 5 = 15
10 - 5 = 5
10 * 5 = 50
10 / 5 = 2
```

Constraints

- Values coming from users will be strings. Ensure that you convert these values to numbers before doing the math.
- Keep the inputs and outputs separate from the numerical conversions and other processing.
- Generate a single output statement with line breaks in the appropriate spots.

Challenges

- Revise the program to ensure that inputs are entered as numeric values. Don't allow the user to proceed if the value entered is not numeric.
- Don't allow the user to enter a negative number.
- Break the program into functions that do the computations. You'll explore functions in Chapter 5, *Functions,* on page 45.
- Implement this program as a GUI program that automatically updates the values when any value changes.

6 Retirement Calculator

Your computer knows what the current year is, which means you can incorporate that into your programs. You just have to figure out how your programming language can provide you with that information.

Create a program that determines how many years you have left until retirement and the year you can retire. It should prompt for your current age and the age you want to retire and display the output as shown in the example that follows.

Example Output

```
What is your current age? 25
At what age would you like to retire? 65
You have 40 years left until you can retire.
It's 2015, so you can retire in 2055.
```

Constraints

- Again, be sure to convert the input to numerical data before doing any math.
- Don't hard-code the current year into your program. Get it from the system time via your programming language.

Challenge

- Handle situations where the program returns a negative number by stating that the user can already retire.

What You Learned

These problems were pretty simple, but hopefully they got you thinking about keeping input, processing, and output separate. When programs are simple, it's tempting to just do some math or string concatenation inside the program's output statements, but as your programs get more complex, you'll find you need to break things into reusable components. You'll be glad you were disciplined from the start.

Head on over to the next chapter. It's time to do some more serious math.

CHAPTER 3

Calculations

You've done some basic math already, but now it's time to dive into more complex math. The exercises in this chapter are a little more challenging. You'll work with formulas for numerical conversion and you'll create some real-world financial programs, too.

These programs will test your knowledge of the order of operations. "Please Excuse My Dear Aunt Sally," or *PEMDAS*, is a common way to remember the order of operations:

- *P*arentheses
- *E*xponents
- *M*ultiplication
- *D*ivision
- *A*ddition
- *S*ubtraction

The computer will always follow these rules, even if you don't want it to. So the exercises in this chapter will have you thinking about adding parentheses to your programs to ensure the output comes out correctly.

You'll want to make good use of test plans for these exercises, too, because you're going to be dealing with precision issues. If you work with decimal numbers in many programming languages, you may encounter some interesting, and unexpected, results. For example, if you add 0.1 and 0.2 in Ruby, you'll get this:

```
> 0.1 + 0.2
 => 0.30000000000000004
```

This happens in JavaScript too. And multiplication can make things even more interesting. Look at this code:

```
> 1.25 * 0.055
 => 0.06875
```

Should that answer be rounded down to 0.06 or up to 0.07? It depends entirely on your business rules. If your answer must be a whole number, you may have to round it up.

Things get even messier with currency. One of the most common issues new programmers face occurs when they try to use floating-point numbers for currency. This will result in precision errors.

One common approach is to represent money using whole numbers. So instead of working with 1.25, work with 125. Do the math, and then shift the decimal back when finished. Here's an example, again in Ruby:

```
> cents = 1.25 * 100.0
 => 125.0
> tax = cents * 0.055
 => 6.875
> tax = tax.round / 100.0
 => 0.07
```

You may need to be a lot more precise than this. These floating-point precision issues exist in many programming languages, and so there are libraries that make working with currency much better. For example, Java has the `BigDecimal` data type that even lets you specify what type of "banker's rounding" you need to do. When you're working on these problems, think carefully about how you need to handle precision. When you do problems for real, especially if it's some kind of financial work, learn how the business you're working with rounds numbers.

One last thing before you dive in: the exercises in this chapter might seem to get a little repetitive toward the end if you're experienced. But for beginners, repetition builds up confidence quickly. It's the same reason you do practice drills in sports or practice your scales over and over in music. By doing several similar problems, you build up your problem-solving skills and improve your speed at breaking down problems. And that translates into success on the job.

7 Area of a Rectangular Room

When working in a global environment, you'll have to present information in both metric and Imperial units. And you'll need to know when to do the conversion to ensure the most accurate results.

Create a program that calculates the area of a room. Prompt the user for the length and width of the room in feet. Then display the area in both square feet and square meters.

Example Output

```
What is the length of the room in feet? 15
What is the width of the room in feet? 20
You entered dimensions of 15 feet by 20 feet.
The area is
300 square feet
27.871 square meters
```

The formula for this conversion is

$$m^2 = f^2 \times 0.09290304$$

Constraints

- Keep the calculations separate from the output.
- Use a constant to hold the conversion factor.

Challenges

- Revise the program to ensure that inputs are entered as numeric values. Don't allow the user to proceed if the value entered is not numeric.
- Create a new version of the program that allows you to choose feet or meters for your inputs.
- Implement this program as a GUI program that automatically updates the values when any value changes.

8 Pizza Party

Division isn't always exact, and sometimes you'll write programs that will need to deal with the leftovers as a whole number instead of a decimal.

Write a program to evenly divide pizzas. Prompt for the number of people, the number of pizzas, and the number of slices per pizza. Ensure that the number of pieces comes out even. Display the number of pieces of pizza each person should get. If there are leftovers, show the number of leftover pieces.

Example Output

```
How many people? 8
How many pizzas do you have? 2

8 people with 2 pizzas
Each person gets 2 pieces of pizza.
There are 0 leftover pieces.
```

Challenges

- Revise the program to ensure that inputs are entered as numeric values. Don't allow the user to proceed if the value entered is not numeric.
- Alter the output so it handles pluralization properly, for example:

  Each person gets 2 pieces of pizza.

  or

  Each person gets 1 piece of pizza.

  Handle the output for leftover pieces appropriately as well.
- Create a variant of the program that prompts for the number of people and the number of pieces each person wants, and calculate how many full pizzas you need to purchase.

9 Paint Calculator

Sometimes you have to round up to the next number rather than follow standard rounding rules.

Calculate gallons of paint needed to paint the ceiling of a room. Prompt for the length and width, and assume one gallon covers 350 square feet. Display the number of gallons needed to paint the ceiling as a *whole number.*

Example Output

```
You will need to purchase 2 gallons of
paint to cover 360 square feet.
```

Remember, you can't buy a partial gallon of paint. You must round up to the next whole gallon.

Constraints

- Use a constant to hold the conversion rate.
- Ensure that you round *up* to the next whole number.

Challenges

- Revise the program to ensure that inputs are entered as numeric values. Don't allow the user to proceed if the value entered is not numeric.
- Implement support for a round room.
- Implement support for an L-shaped room.
- Implement a mobile version of this app so it can be used at the hardware store.

10 Self-Checkout

Working with multiple inputs and currency can introduce some tricky precision issues.

Create a simple self-checkout system. Prompt for the prices and quantities of three items. Calculate the subtotal of the items. Then calculate the tax using a tax rate of 5.5%. Print out the line items with the quantity and total, and then print out the subtotal, tax amount, and total.

Example Output

```
Enter the price of item 1: 25
Enter the quantity of item 1: 2
Enter the price of item 2: 10
Enter the quantity of item 2: 1
Enter the price of item 3: 4
Enter the quantity of item 3: 1
Subtotal: $64.00
Tax: $3.52
Total: $67.52
```

Constraints

- Keep the input, processing, and output parts of your program separate. Collect the input, then do the math operations and string building, and then print out the output.
- Be sure you explicitly convert input to numerical data before doing any calculations.

Challenges

- Revise the program to ensure that prices and quantities are entered as numeric values. Don't allow the user to proceed if the value entered is not numeric.
- Alter the program so that an indeterminate number of items can be entered. The tax and total are computed when there are no more items to be entered.

11 Currency Conversion

At some point, you might have to deal with currency exchange rates, and you'll need to ensure your calculations are as precise as possible.

Write a program that converts currency. Specifically, convert euros to U.S. dollars. Prompt for the amount of money in euros you have, and prompt for the current exchange rate of the euro. Print out the new amount in U.S. dollars. The formula for currency conversion is

$$amount_{to} = \frac{amount_{from} \times rate_{from}}{rate_{to}}$$

where

- *Amount to* is the amount in U.S. dollars.
- *Amount from* is the amount in euros.
- *rate from* is the current exchange rate in euros.
- *rate to* is the current exchange rate of the U.S. dollar.

Example Output

```
How many euros are you exchanging? 81
What is the exchange rate? 137.51
81 euros at an exchange rate of 137.51 is
111.38 U.S. dollars.
```

Constraints

- Ensure that fractions of a cent are rounded up to the next penny.
- Use a single output statement.

Challenges

- Build a dictionary of conversion rates and prompt for the countries instead of the rates.
- Wire up your application to an external API[1] that provides the current exchange rates.

1. https://openexchangerates.org/ is a good example.

12 Computing Simple Interest

Computing simple interest is a great way to quickly figure out whether an investment has value. It's also a good way to get comfortable with explicitly coding the order of operations in your programs.

Create a program that computes simple interest. Prompt for the principal amount, the rate as a percentage, and the time, and display the amount accrued (principal + interest).

The formula for simple interest is $A = P(1 + rt)$, where P is the principal amount, r is the annual rate of interest, t is the number of years the amount is invested, and A is the amount at the end of the investment.

Example Output

```
Enter the principal: 1500
Enter the rate of interest: 4.3
Enter the number of years: 4

After 4 years at 4.3%, the investment will
be worth $1758.
```

Constraints

- Prompt for the rate as a percentage (like 15, not .15). Divide the input by 100 in your program.
- Ensure that fractions of a cent are rounded up to the next penny.
- Ensure that the output is formatted as money.

Challenges

- Ensure that the values entered for principal, rate, and number of years are numeric and that the program will not let the user proceed without valid inputs.
- Alter the program to use a function called `calculateSimpleInterest` that takes in the rate, principal, and number of years and returns the amount at the end of the investment.
- In addition to printing out the final amount, print out the amount at the end of each year.

13 Determining Compound Interest

Simple interest is something you use only when making a quick guess. Most investments use a compound interest formula, which will be much more accurate. And this formula requires you to incorporate exponents into your programs.

Write a program to compute the value of an investment compounded over time. The program should ask for the starting amount, the number of years to invest, the interest rate, and the number of periods per year to compound.

The formula you'll use for this is

$$A = P\left(1 + \frac{r}{n}\right)^{nt}$$

where

- P is the principal amount.
- r is the annual rate of interest.
- t is the number of years the amount is invested.
- n is the number of times the interest is compounded per year.
- A is the amount at the end of the investment.

Example Output

```
What is the principal amount? 1500
What is the rate? 4.3
What is the number of years? 6
What is the number of times the interest
is compounded per year? 4
$1500 invested at 4.3% for 6 years
compounded 4 times per year is $1938.84.
```

Constraints

- Prompt for the rate as a percentage (like 15, not .15). Divide the input by 100 in your program.
- Ensure that fractions of a cent are rounded up to the next penny.
- Ensure that the output is formatted as money.

Challenges

- Ensure that all of the inputs are numeric and that the program will not let the user proceed without valid inputs.
- Create a version of the program that works in reverse, so you can determine the initial amount you'd need to invest to reach a specific goal.
- Implement this program as a GUI app that automatically updates the values when any value changes.

What You Learned

So much of what we do as programmers involves taking some formula and turning it into code. You'll write invoices, reports, tax calculators, currency conversions, and more complex things like computing the distance between two points on a map. Taking a written formula and translating it into an algorithm is not just something you do when you're learning how to code.

We do something else every day as programmers: we make the computer compare values and respond accordingly. Head to the next chapter to tackle those kinds of problems.

CHAPTER 4

Making Decisions

So far, the programs you've worked on have been somewhat simple. But sometimes you need to make a decision based on input from a user. And that's where programming starts to get more challenging. Programs get longer and more complex, and testing them becomes more difficult. This is where test plans become even more important; to ensure correctness, you have to test all the possible ways the input can be interpreted.

So how do you make decisions in your programs? Most programming languages have an if statement where you compare a value to another value. In JavaScript, an if statement looks like this:

```
if (userInput === 'Hello') {
  // do something
}
```

If the input is Hello, then the code between the curly braces runs. This is a simple if statement. If the provided input was anything else, absolutely nothing would happen. Sometimes that's what you want. Other times you may want to do something else, and so you can add an else statement:

```
if (userInput === 'Hello') {
  // do something.
} else {
  // do something else.
}
```

And sometimes you may have more than an either-or situation:

```
if (userInput === 'Hello') {
  // do something.
} else if (userInput === 'Goodbye') {
  // do something different than the first thing.
} else {
  // do something else.
}
```

If you have a lot of possible outcomes, then that might be a great time to use a switch statement:

```
switch(userInput) {
  case: "Hello"
    // do something.
    break;
  case: "Goodbye"
    // do something different than the first thing
    break;
  case: "How was your day?"
    // do something different than the other two things.
    break;
  default:
    // do something else.
}
```

In a larger program, you may have to do different calculations in each part, or multiple steps. It's possible to nest if statements inside other if statements, too, so you may have to do that from time to time. However, overuse of nested if statements can lead to code that's hard to read and even harder to maintain over time. So as you get more comfortable, you'll want to explore different solutions for decision processing.

Writing the code is only a small part of the problem. *Figuring out what code to write* is more difficult. Flowcharts can help you visualize the problem you're solving, and they come in handy when wrapping your mind around decision logic.

For example, if you had to write a program that prompted the user for a number greater than 100, and you needed to display "Thank you" when the number is greater than 100 or "That's not correct" if it's 100 or less, you could create a flowchart like this:

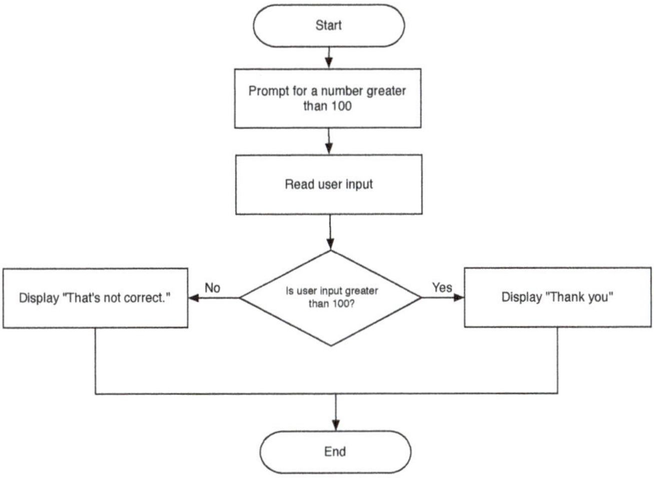

And that flowchart would then be pretty easy to turn into pseudocode:

```
Initialize output to ""
Initialize userInput to ""
Prompt for userInput with "Enter a number greater than 100"

IF userInput is greater than 100 THEN
  output = "Thank you."
ELSE
  output = "That's not correct."
END

Display output
```

This approach can help you understand the problem better and will also help you catch things you missed. Look at the algorithm here. Do you see anything important that I left out?

I forgot to convert the user's input from a string to a number before I compared the values. Some languages would catch that by erroring out, but other languages would keep on going, resulting in a logic error. By writing up a flowchart and pseudocode, I was able to communicate my intention to you quickly so you could see if there were any missing steps or flaws in my logic *before I spent any time writing code.*

As you work through the exercises in this chapter, try to use flowcharts and pseudocode to determine the algorithm for the program, and then turn it into code.

You'll start out solving problems by making simple decisions, such as "if this happens, do this." Next you'll look at how to handle either-or situations. Then you'll have to solve problems that get more complex, where the result of one decision raises another decision. That's where these planning tools will come in handy.

14 Tax Calculator

You don't always need a complex control structure to solve simple problems. Sometimes a program requires an extra step in one case, but in all other cases there's nothing to do.

Write a simple program to compute the tax on an order amount. The program should prompt for the order amount and the state. If the state is "WI," then the order must be charged 5.5% tax. The program should display the subtotal, tax, and total for Wisconsin residents but display just the total for non-residents.

Example Output

```
What is the order amount? 10
What is the state? WI
The subtotal is $10.00.
The tax is $0.55.
The total is $10.55.
```

Or

```
What is the order amount? 10
What is the state? MN
The total is $10.00
```

Constraints

- Implement this program using only a simple `if` statement—don't use an `else` clause.
- Ensure that all money is rounded up to the nearest cent.
- Use a single output statement at the end of the program to display the program results.

Challenges

- Allow the user to enter a state abbreviation in upper, lower, or mixed case.
- Also allow the user to enter the state's full name in upper, lower, or mixed case.

15 Password Validation

Passwords are validated by comparing a user-provided value with a known value that's stored. Either it's correct or it's not.

Create a simple program that validates user login credentials. The program must prompt the user for a username and password. The program should compare the password given by the user to a known password. If the password matches, the program should display "Welcome!" If it doesn't match, the program should display "I don't know you."

Example Output

```
What is the password? 12345
I don't know you.
```

Or

```
What is the password? abc$123
Welcome!
```

Constraints

- Use an if/else statement for this problem.
- Make sure the program is case sensitive.

Challenges

- Investigate how you can prevent the password from being displayed on the screen in clear text when typed.
- Create a map of usernames and passwords and ensure the username and password combinations match.
- Encode the passwords using Bcrypt and store the hashes in the map instead of the clear-text passwords. Then, when you prompt for the password, encrypt the password using Bcrypt and compare it with the value in your map.

16 Legal Driving Age

You can test for equality, but you may need to test to see how a number compares to a known value and display a message if the number is too low or too high.

Write a program that asks the user for their age and compare it to the legal driving age of sixteen. If the user is sixteen or older, then the program should display "You are old enough to legally drive." If the user is under sixteen, the program should display "You are not old enough to legally drive."

Example Output

```
What is your age? 15
You are not old enough to legally drive.
```

Or

```
What is your age? 35
You are old enough to legally drive.
```

Constraints

- Use a single output statement.
- Use a ternary operator to write this program. If your language doesn't support a ternary operator, use a regular if/else statement, and still use a single output statement to display the message.

Challenges

- If the user enters a number that's less than zero or enters non-numeric data, display an error message that asks the user to enter a valid age.
- Instead of hard-coding the driving age in your program logic, research driving ages for various countries and create a lookup table for the driving ages and countries. Prompt for the age, and display which countries the user can legally drive in.

17 Blood Alcohol Calculator

Sometimes you have to perform a more complex calculation based on some provided inputs and then use that result to make a determination.

Create a program that prompts for your weight, gender, number of drinks, the amount of alcohol by volume of the drinks consumed, and the amount of time since your last drink. Calculate your blood alcohol content (BAC) using this formula

$$BAC = (A \times 5.14 / W \times r) - .015 \times H$$

where

- A is total alcohol consumed, in ounces (oz).
- W is body weight in pounds.
- r is the alcohol distribution ratio:
  - 0.73 for men
  - 0.66 for women
- H is number of hours since the last drink.

Display whether or not it's legal to drive by comparing the blood alcohol content to 0.08.

Example Output

```
Your BAC is 0.08
It is not legal for you to drive.
```

Constraint

- Prevent the user from entering non-numeric values.

Challenges

- Handle metric units.
- Look up the legal BAC limit by state and prompt for the state. Display a message that states whether or not it's legal to drive based on the computed BAC.
- Develop this as a mobile application that makes it easy to record each drink, updating the BAC each time a drink is entered.

18 Temperature Converter

You'll often need to determine which part of a program is run based on user input or other events.

Create a program that converts temperatures from Fahrenheit to Celsius or from Celsius to Fahrenheit. Prompt for the starting temperature. The program should prompt for the type of conversion and then perform the conversion.

The formulas are

$$C = (F - 32) \times 5/9$$

and

$$F = (C \times 9/5) + 32$$

Example Output

```
Press C to convert from Fahrenheit to Celsius.
Press F to convert from Celsius to Fahrenheit.
Your choice: C

Please enter the temperature in Fahrenheit: 32
The temperature in Celsius is 0.
```

Constraints

- Ensure that you allow upper or lowercase values for `C` and `F`.
- Use as few output statements as possible and avoid repeating output strings.

Challenges

- Revise the program to ensure that inputs are entered as numeric values. Don't allow the user to proceed if the value entered is not numeric.
- Break the program into functions that perform the computations.
- Implement this program as a GUI program that automatically updates the values when any value changes.
- Modify the program so it also supports the Kelvin scale.

19 BMI Calculator

You'll often need to see if one value is within a certain range and alter the flow of a program as a result.

Create a program to calculate the body mass index (BMI) for a person using the person's height in inches and weight in pounds. The program should prompt the user for weight and height.

Calculate the BMI by using the following formula:

$$bmi = (weight / (height \times height)) * 703$$

If the BMI is between 18.5 and 25, display that the person is at a normal weight. If they are out of that range, tell them if they are underweight or overweight and tell them to consult their doctor.

Example Output

```
Your BMI is 19.5.
You are within the ideal weight range.
```

or

```
Your BMI is 32.5.
You are overweight. You should see your doctor.
```

Constraint

- Ensure your program takes only numeric data. Don't let the user continue unless the data is valid.

Challenges

- Make the user interface accept height and weight in Imperial or metric units. You'll need a slightly different formula for metric units.
- For Imperial measurements, prompt for feet and inches and convert feet to inches so the user doesn't have to.
- Use a GUI interface with sliders for height and weight. Update the user interface on the fly. Use colors as well as text to indicate health.

20 Multistate Sales Tax Calculator

More complex programs may have decisions nested in other decisions, so that when one decision is made, additional decisions must be made.

Create a tax calculator that handles multiple states and multiple counties within each state. The program prompts the user for the order amount and the state where the order will be shipped.

For Wisconsin residents, prompt for the county of residence.

- For Eau Claire county residents, add an additional 0.005 tax.
- For Dunn county residents, add an additional 0.004 tax.

Illinois residents must be charged 8% sales tax with no additional county-level charge. All other states are not charged tax. The program then displays the tax and the total for Wisconsin and Illinois residents but just the total for everyone else.

Example Output

```
What is the order amount? 10
What state do you live in? Wisconsin
The tax is $0.50.
The total is $10.50.
```

Constraints

- Ensure that all money is rounded up to the nearest cent.
- Use a single output statement at the end of the program to display the program results.

Challenges

- Add support for your state and county.
- Allow the user to enter a state abbreviation and county name in upper, lower, or mixed case.
- Allow the user to also enter the state's full name in upper, lower, or mixed case.
- Implement the program using data structures to avoid nested `if` statements.

21 Numbers to Names

Many programs display information to the end user in one form but use a different form inside the program. For example, you may show the word *Blue* on the screen, but behind the scenes you'll have a numerical value for that color or an internal value because you may need to represent the textual description in another language for Spanish-speaking visitors.

Write a program that converts a number from 1 to 12 to the corresponding month. Prompt for a number and display the corresponding calendar month, with 1 being January and 12 being December. For any value outside that range, display an appropriate error message.

Example Output

```
Please enter the number of the month: 3
The name of the month is March.
```

Constraints

- Use a `switch` or `case` statement for this program.
- Use a single output statement for this program.

Challenges

- Use a map or dictionary to remove the `switch` statement from the program.
- Support multiple languages. Prompt for the language at the beginning of the program.

22 Comparing Numbers

Comparing one input to a known value is common enough, but you'll often need to process a collection of inputs.

Write a program that asks for three numbers. Check first to see that all numbers are different. If they're not different, then exit the program. Otherwise, display the largest number of the three.

Example Output

```
Enter the first number: 1
Enter the second number: 51
Enter the third number: 2
The largest number is 51.
```

Constraint

- Write the algorithm manually. Don't use a built-in function for finding the largest number in a list.

Challenges

- Modify the program so that all entered values are tracked and the user is prevented from entering a number that's already been entered.
- Modify the program so that it asks for ten numbers instead of three.
- Modify the program so that it asks for an unlimited number of numbers.

23 Troubleshooting Car Issues

An *expert system* is a type of artificial intelligence program that uses a knowledge base and a set of rules to perform a task that a human expert might do. Many websites are available that will help you self-diagnose a medical issue by answering a series of questions. And many hardware and software companies offer online troubleshooting tools to help people solve simple technical issues before calling a human.

Create a program that walks the user through troubleshooting issues with a car. Use the following decision tree to build the system:

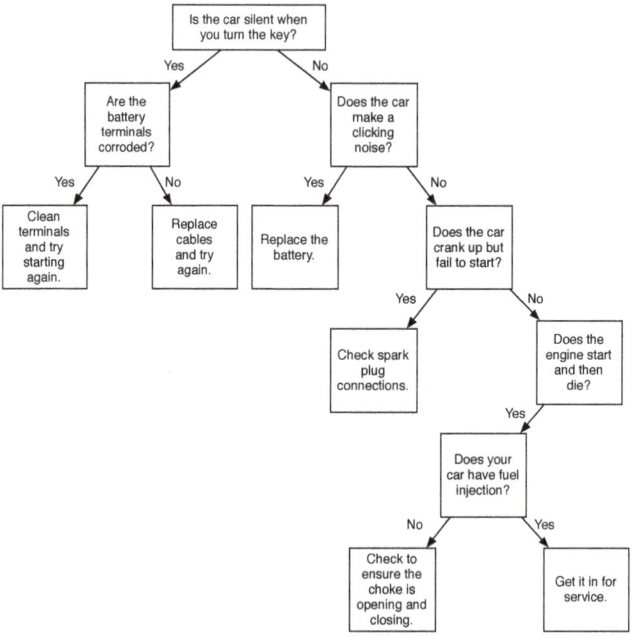

Example Output

```
Is the car silent when you turn the key? y
Are the battery terminals corroded? n
The battery cables may be damaged.
Replace cables and try again.
```

Constraint

- Ask only questions that are relevant to the situation and to the previous answers. Don't ask for all inputs at once.

Challenge

- Investigate rules engines and inference engines. These are powerful ways to solve complex problems that are based on rules and facts. Identify a rules engine for your programming language and use it to solve this problem.

What You Learned

Decision processing is a critical part of software development. It's what drives menu systems. It's what determines whether the onscreen avatar jumps, runs, or shoots when you press a key. And, when actually implemented, it's what translates obscure error codes into error messages that a human can understand.

But as you worked through these programs, you probably noticed you had to do a lot more testing than you did with the previous programs because there were more possible outputs. The more you branch in your code, the more possible outcomes you'll have.

Before moving on, double-check the logic in your programs. Did you cover all the possible outcomes? For that BMI calculator, what if the BMI ends up right on the line? Did you use the right comparison operator?

When you're confident that your code is flawless, move on to the next chapter and start incorporating functions into your programs.

CHAPTER 5

Functions

Our programs are getting complex. Even if we try to separate our input, processing, and output, as programs get more complex, it gets harder and harder to find things.

But we can use functions to organize our code, and we can even create reusable components.

Functions act like smaller programs inside our main program. Here's some JavaScript code that defines a function that adds two numbers:

```
function addTwoNumbers(firstNumber, secondNumber) {
  return(
    firstNumber + secondNumber
  );
}
```

The addTwoNumbers function takes in two numbers as its input, does the calculation, and returns the result to the rest of the program. Here's how to use it:

```
var sum = addTwoNumbers(1,2);
console.log(sum);
```

Another benefit of functions is that the logic is encapsulated in the body of the function, and it can be changed without affecting the programs that use it. For example, our function takes in two values, but if we called it like this

```
var sum = addTwoNumbers("1","2");
console.log(sum);
```

then the program's output would be 12, because JavaScript will concatenate strings instead of converting them to numbers. But we can modify the addTwoNumbers function to convert the input to numbers automatically so the function will always work.

Often, we'll take the result of one function and send it on to another function. Or we'll evaluate the result of a function to make a decision. Some programming languages are based entirely on functions, like Elixir and Clojure. Those are the aptly named *functional* programming languages.

When solving the problems in this chapter, organize your code into functions. Try to encapsulate the main algorithm into a function that you invoke from the rest of your program. Or go further and create functions that capture the input and construct the output.

This chapter is intentionally short, because when you finish these exercises, you should revisit your previous programs and see how functions can improve the organization of those programs as well.

24 Anagram Checker

Using functions to abstract the logic away from the rest of your code makes it easier to read and easier to maintain.

Create a program that compares two strings and determines if the two strings are anagrams. The program should prompt for both input strings and display the output as shown in the example that follows.

Example Output

```
Enter two strings and I'll tell you if they
are anagrams:
Enter the first string: note
Enter the second string: tone
"note" and "tone" are anagrams.
```

Constraints

- Implement the program using a function called `isAnagram`, which takes in two words as its arguments and returns `true` or `false`. Invoke this function from your main program.
- Check that both words are the same length.

Challenge

- Complete this program without using built-in language features. Use selection or repetition logic instead and develop your own algorithm.

25 Password Strength Indicator

Functions help you abstract away complex operations, but they also help you build reusable components.

Create a program that determines the complexity of a given password based on these rules:

- A very weak password contains only numbers and is fewer than eight characters.
- A weak password contains only letters and is fewer than eight characters.
- A strong password contains letters and at least one number and is at least eight characters.
- A very strong password contains letters, numbers, and special characters and is at least eight characters.

Example Output

```
The password '12345' is a very weak password.
The password 'abcdef' is a weak password.
The password 'abc123xyz' is a strong password.
The password '1337h@xor!' is a very strong password.
```

Constraints

- Create a passwordValidator function that takes in the password as its argument and returns a value you can evaluate to determine the password strength. Do not have the function return a string—you may need to support multiple languages in the future.
- Use a single output statement.

Challenge

- Create a GUI application or web application that displays graphical feedback as well as text feedback in real time. As someone enters a password, determine its strength and display the result.

26 Months to Pay Off a Credit Card

It can take a lot longer to pay off your credit card balance than you might realize. And the formula for figuring that out isn't pretty. Hiding the formula's complexity with a function can help you keep your code organized.

Write a program that will help you determine how many months it will take to pay off a credit card balance. The program should ask the user to enter the balance of a credit card and the APR of the card. The program should then return the number of months needed.

The formula for this is

$$n = -\frac{1}{30} \times \frac{\log\left(1 + \frac{b}{p}\left(1 - (1 + i)^{30}\right)\right)}{\log(1 + i)}$$

where

- n is the number of months.
- i is the daily rate (APR divided by 365).
- b is the balance.
- p is the monthly payment.

Example Output

```
What is your balance? 5000
What is the APR on the card (as a percent)? 12
What is the monthly payment you can make? 100

It will take you 70 months to pay off this card.
```

Constraints

- Prompt for the card's APR. Do the division internally.
- Prompt for the APR as a percentage, not a decimal.
- Use a function called calculateMonthsUntilPaidOff, which accepts the balance, the APR, and the monthly payment as its arguments and returns the number of months. Don't access any of these values outside the function.
- Round fractions of a cent up to the next cent.

Challenge

- Rework the formula so the program can accept the number of months as an input and compute the monthly payment. Create a version of the program that lets the user choose whether to figure out the number of months until payoff or the amount needed to pay per month.

27 Validating Inputs

Large functions aren't very usable or maintainable. It makes a lot of sense to break down the logic of a program into smaller functions that do one thing each. The program can then call these functions in sequence to perform the work.

Write a program that prompts for a first name, last name, employee ID, and ZIP code. Ensure that the input is valid according to these rules:

- The first name must be filled in.
- The last name must be filled in.
- The first and last names must be at least two characters long.
- An employee ID is in the format AA-1234. So, two letters, a hyphen, and four numbers.
- The ZIP code must be a number.

Display appropriate error messages on incorrect data.

Example Output

```
Enter the first name: J
Enter the last name:
Enter the ZIP code: ABCDE
Enter an employee ID:  A12-1234
"J" is not a valid first name. It is too short.
The last name must be filled in.
The ZIP code must be numeric.
A12-1234 is not a valid ID.
```

Or

```
Enter the first name: Jimmy
Enter the last name: James
Enter the ZIP code: 55555
Enter an employee ID:  TK-421
There were no errors found.
```

Constraints

- Create a function for each type of validation you need to write. Then create a validateInput function that takes in all of the input data and invokes the specific validation functions.
- Use a single output statement to display the outputs.

Challenges

- Use regular expressions to validate the input.
- Implement this as a GUI application or web application that gives immediate feedback when the fields lose focus.
- Repeat the process if the input is not valid.

What You Learned

Now it's time to go back through the previous chapters and revisit the exercises there. Locate the main algorithm of the program and encapsulate it in a function. And see if it's helpful to break one function into smaller functions. After all, nothing says you can't call one function from another. Then see if you're repeating some functions in your programs. Look into ways you can reuse those functions without copying the code from program to program.

When you're ready to move on, head to the next chapter, where you'll find some problems that will require you to make the computer repeat a process over and over.

CHAPTER 6

Repetition

How do you make a computer do the same thing over and over again? Surely you don't have to type the code multiple times, right?

According to the structured program theorem, you can use three basic control structures to solve problems with computer programs: sequencing, selection, and repetition. *Sequencing* is a fancy way of saying that you need to process one step after another in the right order. And *selection* is making decisions based on conditions. We've done both of these throughout the book already. Our early programs did a lot of sequencing, and then we moved into selection when we had our programs start making decisions based on conditions.

But in order to repeat parts of our programs without duplicating code, we use *repetition,* where we specify that a set of instructions should repeat as long as a condition is true. Think of it as "Keep asking for input while the user wants to enter more values," or "Do these five steps over and over until you have no records left."

How we do this repetition depends on the result we want. We may want to repeat a certain number of times, or once for each item in a list of names, or until the user tells us we're finished.

The programming language you use will influence how you go about solving your problems. For example, in Go, if you wanted to count from 5 down to 1, you'd write code like this:

```
counter := 5
for counter <= 1 {
  fmt.Println(counter)
  counter--;
}
```

You start the counter at 5, print it out, and subtract 1. The code keeps going until the counter is less than or equal to 1.

C-style languages like JavaScript have a for loop that lets you define the counter variable and the incrementation as part of the declaration of the loop:

```
for(var counter = 5; counter <= 1; counter--) {
  console.log(counter);
}
```

A Ruby developer might approach this differently; in Ruby, integers are objects that support repetition:

```
5.times do |counter|
  # counter is 0-based.
  puts 5 - counter
end
```

But some languages, like Elixir, don't have loops and instead rely on recursion:

```
defmodule Recursion do
  def loop(n) when n <= 1, do: IO.puts n

  def loop(n) do
    IO.puts n
    loop(n - 1)
  end
end

loop(5)
```

Recursion occurs when a function calls itself, either directly or indirectly. In the preceding example, the loop function calls itself, subtracting 1 each time until n is less than 1. Not every language is optimized for recursion though; if you make a function call itself too many times in some languages, it'll make too many copies of itself and fill up the stack, crashing the program. So once again, the programming language you choose determines the approach you'll take.

These examples are all counted loops, where you count up or down to a known value. But other times you may need a different reason to stop. You might stop when a certain value is entered:

```
var value;
var keepGoing = true;
while(keepGoing) {
  value =  prompt("Enter a number or 0 to stop.");
  keepGoing = value !== 0;
  // more stuff
}
```

Or you might keep going while there are more lines in the file to process or while there are more records from the database to display.

The exercises in this chapter will require you to use repetition to get them to work efficiently. As you read each program's problem statement, think carefully about whether you're being asked to do something a specific number of times or an unknown number of times. Then pick the most appropriate approach.

You may find that using flowcharts will help you determine the logic. Remember our program in Chapter 4, *Making Decisions,* on page 29 where we used a flowchart to help with the logic? We had to prompt for a number greater than 100. We ended the program if we didn't get the input we wanted. But we could use repetition to keep asking, and we can use a flowchart to represent that logic:

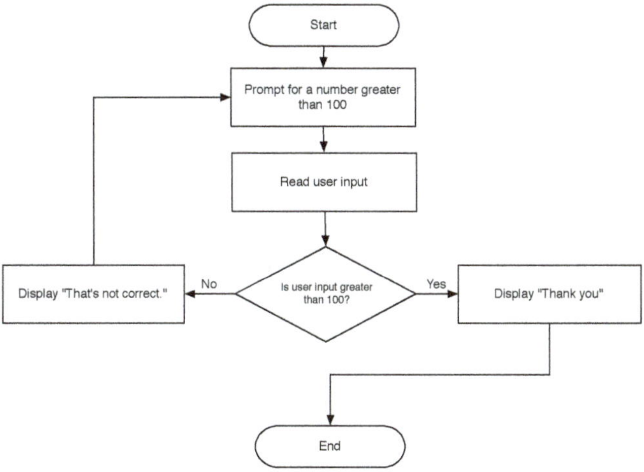

This flowchart helps clarify that the program contains a repeating process; when the user enters an incorrect value, we prompt them again. From here we can determine the best way to implement that process with our code.

The exercises in this chapter are somewhat simplistic, but they'll help you get ready for the chapters that follow, which will rely heavily on repetition. Work through these to get the solid grounding you need.

28 Adding Numbers

In previous programs, you asked the user for repeated input by writing the input statements multiple times. But it's more efficient to use loops to deal with repeated input.

Write a program that prompts the user for five numbers and computes the total of the numbers.

Example Output

```
Enter a number: 1
Enter a number: 2
Enter a number: 3
Enter a number: 4
Enter a number: 5
The total is 15.
```

Constraints

- The prompting must use repetition, such as a counted loop, not three separate prompts.
- Create a flowchart before writing the program.

Challenges

- Modify the program to prompt for how many numbers to add, instead of hard-coding the value. Be sure you convert the input to a number before doing the comparison.
- Modify the program so that it only adds numbers and silently rejects non-numeric values. Count these invalid entries as attempts anyway. In other words, if the number of numbers to add is 5, your program should still prompt only five times.

29 Handling Bad Input

The rule of 72 is a quick method for estimating how long it will take to double your investment, by taking the number 72 and dividing it by the expected rate of return. It's a good tool that helps you figure out if the stock, bond, or savings account is right for you. It's also a good program to write to test for and prevent bad input because computers can't divide by zero. And instead of exiting the program when the user enters invalid input, you can just keep prompting for inputs until you get one that's valid.

Write a quick calculator that prompts for the rate of return on an investment and calculates how many years it will take to double your investment.

The formula is

$$years = 72 / r$$

where r is the stated rate of return.

Example Output

```
What is the rate of return? 0
Sorry. That's not a valid input.
What is the rate of return? ABC
Sorry. That's not a valid input.
What is the rate of return? 4
It will take 18 years to double your initial investment.
```

Constraints

- Don't allow the user to enter 0.
- Don't allow non-numeric values.
- Use a loop to trap bad input, so you can ensure that the user enters valid values.

Challenge

- Display a different error message when the user enters 0.

30 Multiplication Table

Create a program that generates multiplication tables for the numbers 0 through 12.

Example Output

```
0 X 0 = 0
0 X 1 = 0
....
12 x 11 = 132
12 x 12 = 144
```

Constraint

- Use a nested loop to complete this program.

Challenges

- Create a graphical program. Use a drop-down list to change the base number. Generate or update the table when the number is selected.
- Generate a single multiplication table like the following:

	0	1	2	3	4	5	6	7	8	9	10	11	12
0	0	0	0	0	0	0	0	0	0	0	0	0	0
1	0	1	2	3	4	5	6	7	8	9	10	11	12
2	0	2	4	6	8	10	12	14	16	18	20	22	24
3	0	3	6	9	12	15	18	21	24	27	30	33	36
4	0	4	8	12	16	20	24	28	32	36	40	44	48
5	0	5	10	15	20	25	30	35	40	45	50	55	60
6	0	6	12	18	24	30	36	42	48	54	60	66	72
7	0	7	14	21	28	35	42	49	56	63	70	77	84
8	0	8	16	24	32	40	48	56	64	72	80	88	96
9	0	9	18	27	36	45	54	63	72	81	90	99	108
10	0	10	20	30	40	50	60	70	80	90	100	110	120
11	0	11	22	33	44	55	66	77	88	99	110	121	132
12	0	12	24	36	48	60	72	84	96	108	120	132	144

31 Karvonen Heart Rate

When you loop, you can control how much you increment the counter; you don't always have to increment by one.

When getting into a fitness program, you may want to figure out your target heart rate so you don't overexert yourself. The Karvonen heart rate formula is one method you can use to determine your rate. Create a program that prompts for your age and your resting heart rate. Use the Karvonen formula to determine the target heart rate based on a range of intensities from 55% to 95%. Generate a table with the results as shown in the example output. The formula is

$$TargetHeartRate = (((220 - age) - restingHR) \times intensity) + restingHR$$

Example Output

```
Resting Pulse: 65    Age: 22

Intensity      | Rate
---------------|--------
55%            | 138 bpm
60%            | 145 bpm
65%            | 151 bpm
 :               :        (extra lines omitted)
85%            | 178 bpm
90%            | 185 bpm
95%            | 191 bpm
```

Constraints

- Don't hard-code the percentages. Use a loop to increment the percentages from 55 to 95.
- Ensure that the heart rate and age are entered as numbers. Don't allow the user to continue without entering valid inputs.
- Display the results in a tabular format.

Challenge

- Implement this as a GUI program that allows the user to use a slider control for the intensity, and update the interface in real time as the slider moves.

32 Guess the Number Game

Write a Guess the Number game that has three levels of difficulty. The first level of difficulty would be a number between 1 and 10. The second difficulty set would be between 1 and 100. The third difficulty set would be between 1 and 1000.

Prompt for the difficulty level, and then start the game. The computer picks a random number in that range and prompts the player to guess that number. Each time the player guesses, the computer should give the player a hint as to whether the number is too high or too low. The computer should also keep track of the number of guesses. Once the player guesses the correct number, the computer should present the number of guesses and ask if the player would like to play again.

Example Output

```
Let's play Guess the Number.
Pick a difficulty level (1, 2, or 3): 1
I have my number. What's your guess? 1
Too low.  Guess again: 5
Too high. Guess again: 2
You got it in 3 guesses!
Play again? n
Goodbye!
```

Constraints

- Don't allow any non-numeric data entry.
- During the game, count non-numeric entries as wrong guesses.

Challenges

- Map the number of guesses taken to comments:
  - 1 guess: "You're a mind reader!"
  - 2–4 guesses: "Most impressive."
  - 3–6 guesses: "You can do better than that."
  - 7 or more guesses: "Better luck next time."

- Keep track of previous guesses and issue an alert that the user has already guessed that number. Count this as a wrong guess.
- Implement this as a graphical game with a grid of numbers. When a number is clicked or tapped, remove the number from the screen.

What You Learned

At this point you should be pretty confident in your abilities. You've mastered conditional logic, you know how to use functions, and now you can make parts of your programs repeat. You can even trap bad input. Many of the previous programs in this book can benefit from what you've learned, so before moving on, modify a few of those programs. Perhaps start by preventing invalid input on some of the calculation programs.

This chapter was short because you really can't do a lot of real-world problems without first understanding data structures like arrays. And so that's what the next chapter is all about. Let's go!

CHAPTER 7

Data Structures

Only the simplest programs can get away with storing data in variables. But these next programs will get you to think about storing data in lists or name/value pairs, or even a combination of the two.

Depending on the language you choose, you might be looking for *arrays, lists, hashes, hashmaps, dictionaries, associative arrays,* or *maps.* And while languages have different names, the concepts are the same. You group data together using data structures. To keep it simple, I'm going to use the terms *array* and *map*.

An array is a data structure that holds a list of values:

```
colors = ["Red", "Green", "Blue"];
```

Usually, the order of items in the array is preserved. To get a value out, you access it by its index, which is a reference to the item's position in the array. In most languages, the first item is at index 0:

```
colors = ["Red", "Green", "Blue"];
console.log(colors[0]);
>> "Red"
```

A map is a data structure that maps keys to values, and you retrieve data by the key rather than the position:

```
person = {name: "Homer", age: 42};
console.log person["name"];
```

One of the most common uses of data structures is representing a collection of records from a database. Each record is represented by a map, with each field being a name/value pair within the map. The collection of records is represented by an array.

Here's an example in JavaScript:

```
var people = [
  {name: "Homer", age: 42},
  {name: "Barney", age: 41}
]
```

And here's the same structure, but written in Elixir:

```
people = [
  %{name: "Homer", age: 42},
  %{name: "Barney", age: 41}
]
```

While the syntax is different, the concept is the same; you use data structures to store similar data so you can use it in your programs.

Data structures are often used in conjunction with loops. For example, if you had a list of names and you wanted to print each one, you would iterate over the collection and sum up the values. Here's a quick example in JavaScript using a for loop:

```
var names = ["Ted", "Barney", "Carl", "Tracy"];
for(var i = 0, length = names.length; i < length; i++) {
  console.log(names[i]);
}
```

However, many languages offer an alternative approach. In Ruby, you can write the same code like this:

```
names = ["Ted", "Barney", "Carl", "Tracy"]
names.each { |name| puts name }
```

Elixir offers a similar approach:

```
names = ["Ted", "Barney", "Carl", "Tracy"]
names
  |> Enum.each fn(name) -> IO.puts name end
```

Java, C#, JavaScript, and many other languages have lots of features for iterating, sorting, and manipulating lists and other data structures. So as you work through this chapter, look up how to work with these concepts and use what you learn to solve the problems in this chapter.

33 Magic 8 Ball

Arrays are great for storing possible responses from a program. If you combine that with a random number generator, you can pick a random entry from this list, which works great for games.

Create a Magic 8 Ball game that prompts for a question and then displays either "Yes," "No," "Maybe," or "Ask again later."

Example Output

```
What's your question?  Will I be rich and famous?
Ask again later.
```

Constraint

- The value should be chosen randomly using a pseudo random number generator. Store the possible choices in a list and select one at random.

Challenges

- Implement this as a GUI application.
- If available, use native device libraries to allow you to "shake" the 8 ball.

34 Employee List Removal

Sometimes you have to locate and remove an entry from a list based on some criteria. You may have a deck of cards and need to discard one so it's no longer in play, or you may need to remove values from a list of valid inputs once they've been used. Storing the values in an array makes this process easier. Depending on your language, you may find it safer and more efficient to create a new array instead of modifying the existing one.

Create a small program that contains a list of employee names. Print out the list of names when the program runs the first time. Prompt for an employee name and remove that specific name from the list of names. Display the remaining employees, each on its own line.

Example Output

```
There are 5 employees:
John Smith
Jackie Jackson
Chris Jones
Amanda Cullen
Jeremy Goodwin

Enter an employee name to remove: Chris Jones

There are 4 employees:
John Smith
Jackie Jackson
Amanda Cullen
Jeremy Goodwin
```

Constraint

- Use an array or list to store the names.

Challenges

- If the user enters a name that's not found, print out an error message stating that the name does not exist.
- Read in the list of employees from a file, with each employee on its own line.
- Write the output to the *same* file you read in.

35 Picking a Winner

Arrays don't have to be hard-coded. You can take user input and store it in an array and then work with it.

Create a program that picks a winner for a contest or prize drawing. Prompt for names of contestants until the user leaves the entry blank. Then randomly select a winner.

Example Output

```
Enter a name: Homer
Enter a name: Bart
Enter a name: Maggie
Enter a name: Lisa
Enter a name: Moe
Enter a name:
The winner is... Maggie.
```

Constraints

- Use a loop to capture user input into an array.
- Use a random number generator to pluck a value from the array.
- Don't include a blank entry in the array.
- Some languages require that you define the length of the array ahead of time. You may need to find another data structure, like an ArrayList.

Challenges

- When a winner is chosen, remove the winner from the list of contestants and allow more winners to be chosen.
- Make a GUI program that shows the array of names being shuffled on the screen before a winner is chosen.
- Create a separate contest registration application. Use this program to pull in all registered users and pick a winner.

36 Computing Statistics

Statistics is important in our field. When measuring response times or rendering times, it's helpful to collect data so you can easily spot abnormalities. For example, the standard deviation helps you determine which values are outliers and which values are within normal ranges.

Write a program that prompts for response times from a website in milliseconds. It should keep asking for values until the user enters "done."

The program should print the average time (mean), the minimum time, the maximum time, and the standard deviation.

To compute the average (mean)

1. Compute the sum of all values.
2. Divide the sum by the number of values.

To compute the standard deviation

1. Calculate the difference from the mean for each number and square it.
2. Compute the mean of the squared values.
3. Take the square root of the mean.

Example Output

```
Enter a number: 100
Enter a number: 200
Enter a number: 1000
Enter a number: 300
Enter a number: done
Numbers: 100, 200, 1000, 300
The average is 400.
The minimum is 100.
The maximum is 1000.
The standard deviation is 400.25.
```

Constraints

- Use loops and arrays to perform the input and mathematical operations.

- Be sure to exclude the "done" entry from the array of inputs.
- Be sure to properly convert numeric values to strings.
- Keep the input separate from the processing and the output.

Challenges

- Use functions called mean, max, min, and standardDeviation, which take in an array of numbers and return the results.
- Have the program read in numbers from an external file instead of prompting for the values.

37 Password Generator

Coming up with a password that meets specific requirements is something your computer can do. And it will give you practice using random number generators in conjunction with a list of known values.

Create a program that generates a secure password. Prompt the user for the minimum length, the number of special characters, and the number of numbers. Then generate a password for the user using those inputs.

Example Output

```
What's the minimum length? 8
How many special characters? 2
How many numbers? 2
Your password is
aurn2$1s#
```

Constraints

- Use lists to store the characters you'll use to generate the passwords.
- Add some randomness to the password generation.

Challenges

- Randomly convert vowels to numbers, such as 3 for `E` and 4 for `A`.
- Have the program present a few options rather than a single result.
- Place the password on the user's clipboard when generated.

38 Filtering Values

Sometimes input you collect will need to be filtered down. Data structures and loops can make this process easier.

Create a program that prompts for a list of numbers, separated by spaces. Have the program print out a new list containing only the even numbers.

Example Output

```
Enter a list of numbers, separated by spaces:  1 2 3 4 5 6 7 8
The even numbers are 2 4 6 8.
```

Constraints

- Convert the input to an array. Many languages can easily convert strings to arrays with a built-in function that splits apart a string based on a specified delimiter.
- Write your own algorithm—don't rely on the language's built-in filter or similar enumeration feature.
- Use a function called filterEvenNumbers to encapsulate the logic for this. The function takes in the old array and returns the new array.

Challenge

- Instead of prompting for numbers, read in lines from any text file and print out only the even-numbered lines.

39 Sorting Records

When you're looking at results, you'll want to be able to sort them so you can find what you're looking for quickly or do some quick visual comparisons.

Given the following data set

First Name	Last Name	Position	Separation date
John	Johnson	Manager	2016-12-31
Tou	Xiong	Software Engineer	2016-10-05
Michaela	Michaelson	District Manager	2015-12-19
Jake	Jacobson	Programmer	
Jacquelyn	Jackson	DBA	
Sally	Weber	Web Developer	2015-12-18

create a program that sorts all employees by last name and prints them to the screen in a tabular format.

Example Output

```
Name                | Position          | Separation Date
--------------------|-------------------|----------------
Jacquelyn Jackson   | DBA               |
Jake Jacobson       | Programmer        |
John Johnson        | Manager           | 2016-12-31
Michaela Michaelson | District Manager  | 2015-12-19
Sally Weber         | Web Developer     | 2015-12-18
Tou Xiong           | Software Engineer | 2016-10-05
```

Constraint

- Implement the data using a list of maps.

Challenges

- Prompt for how the records should be sorted. Allow sorting by separation date, position, or last name.
- Use a database such as MySQL, or a key-value store such as Redis, to store the employee records. Retrieve the records from the data store.

40 Filtering Records

Sorting records is helpful, but sometimes you need to filter down the results to find or display only what you're looking for.

Given the following data set

First Name	Last Name	Position	Separation date
John	Johnson	Manager	2016-12-31
Tou	Xiong	Software Engineer	2016-10-05
Michaela	Michaelson	District Manager	2015-12-19
Jake	Jacobson	Programmer	
Jacquelyn	Jackson	DBA	
Sally	Weber	Web Developer	2015-12-18

create a program that lets a user locate all records that match the search string by comparing the search string to the first or last name field.

Example Output

```
Enter a search string:  Jac

Results:
Name                | Position          | Separation Date
--------------------|-------------------|----------------
Jacquelyn Jackson   | DBA               |
Jake Jacobson       | Programmer        |
```

Constraint

- Implement the data using an array of maps or an associative array.

Challenges

- Make the search case insensitive.
- Add the option to search by position.
- Add the option to find all employees where their separation date is six months ago or more.
- Read in the data from a file.

What You Learned

Data structures help you structure data. You'll find that arrays and maps are *everywhere*. When you work with databases, your records will be returned to you as an array that you'll have to loop through. When you want to read or modify configuration files, you're going to work with arrays and maps. I've lost count of the number of times I've been asked to take an array of data and sort it somehow. And you will too.

Lists and maps are a great start, but you can define your own data structures, too, like a ShoppingCart.

So far we've gotten our data from the user, or we've coded it up ourselves. But in the next chapter, you're going to get your data from files.

CHAPTER 8

Working with Files

All the programs you've worked with so far have taken input from the end user or used hard-coded values. But many programs use files to store data. Your operating system and its programs write logs to files constantly, as do the websites you visit. And many apps use files to hold configuration data. Games use files to store your saved data when you reach a checkpoint.

Even programming languages, like the one you're using to work through this book, work with files. You type your source code into a file, and a compiler or interpreter turns what you wrote into something the computer can run.

The exercises in this chapter ask you to work with files and folders, and you'll need to investigate how to do this in your programming language. Some languages have built-in features to read from a file. Others don't have the features built in but do have libraries you can use to work with files.

You'll want to investigate different approaches, too. You might find that your program performs faster if you can process the file line by line or as a stream of data. Some files are just too big to load all at once, but some situations may require you to read the whole file first before you can process it.

One quick note: if you're using JavaScript inside the web browser, you won't be able to do these exercises without modification because browsers prevent you from reading and writing to the local file system. You can use Node.js instead.

41 Name Sorter

Alphabetizing the contents of a file, or sorting its contents, is a great way to get comfortable manipulating a file in your program.

Create a program that reads in the following list of names:

```
Ling, Mai
Johnson, Jim
Zarnecki, Sabrina
Jones, Chris
Jones, Aaron
Swift, Geoffrey
Xiong, Fong
```

Read this program and sort the list alphabetically. Then print the sorted list to a file that looks like the following example output.

Example Output

```
Total of 7 names
-----------------
Ling, Mai
Johnson, Jim
Jones, Aaron
Jones, Chris
Swift, Geoffrey
Xiong, Fong
Zarnecki, Sabrina
```

Constraint

- Don't hard-code the number of names.

Challenges

- Implement this program by reading in the names from the user, one at a time, and printing out the sorted results to a file.
- Use the program to sort data from a large data set and see how well it performs.
- Implement this program in a functional programming language and compare the programs.

42 Parsing a Data File

Sometimes data comes in as a structured format that you have to break down and turn into records so you can process them. CSV, or comma-separated values, is a common standard for doing this.

Construct a program that reads in the following data file:

```
Ling,Mai,55900
Johnson,Jim,56500
Jones,Aaron,46000
Jones,Chris,34500
Swift,Geoffrey,14200
Xiong,Fong,65000
Zarnecki,Sabrina,51500
```

Process the records and display the results formatted as a table, evenly spaced, as shown in the example output.

Example Output

```
Last     First     Salary
-------------------------
Ling     Mai       55900
Johnson  Jim       56500
Jones    Aaron     46000
Jones    Chris     34500
Swift    Geoffrey  14200
Xiong    Fong      65000
Zarnecki Sabrina   51500
```

Constraints

- Write your own code to parse the data. Don't use a CSV parser.
- Use spaces to align the columns.
- Make each column one space longer than the longest value in the column.

Challenges

- Format the salary as currency with dollar signs and commas.
- Sort the results by salary from highest to lowest.
- Rework your program to use a CSV parsing library and compare the results.

43 Website Generator

Programming languages can create files and folders too.

Create a program that generates a website skeleton with the following specifications:

- Prompt for the name of the site.
- Prompt for the author of the site.
- Ask if the user wants a folder for JavaScript files.
- Ask if the user wants a folder for CSS files.
- Generate an index.html file that contains the name of the site inside the <title> tag and the author in a <meta> tag.

Example Output

```
Site name: awesomeco
Author: Max Power
Do you want a folder for JavaScript? y
Do you want a folder for CSS? y
Created ./awesomeco
Created ./awesomeco/index.html
Created ./awesomeco/js/
Created ./awesomeco/css/
```

Challenges

- Implement this in a scripting language on Windows, OSX, and Linux.
- Implement this as a web application that provides the specified site as a zip file.

44 Product Search

Pulling data from a file into a complex data structure makes parsing much simpler. Many programming languages support the JSON format, a popular way of representing data.

Create a program that takes a product name as input and retrieves the current price and quantity for that product. The product data is in a data file in the JSON format and looks like this:

```
{
  "products" : [
    {"name": "Widget", "price": 25.00, "quantity": 5 },
    {"name": "Thing", "price": 15.00, "quantity": 5 },
    {"name": "Doodad", "price": 5.00, "quantity": 10 }
  ]
}
```

Print out the product name, price, and quantity if the product is found. If no product matches the search, state that no product was found and start over.

Example Output

```
What is the product name? iPad
Sorry, that product was not found in our inventory.
What is the product name? Widget
Name: Widget
Price: $25.00
Quantity on hand: 5
```

Constraints

- The file is in the JSON format. Use a JSON parser to pull the values out of the file.
- If no record is found, prompt again.

Challenges

- Ensure that the product search is case insensitive.
- When a product is not found, ask if the product should be added. If yes, ask for the price and the quantity, and save it in the JSON file. Ensure the newly added product is immediately available for searching without restarting the program.

45 Word Finder

There will be times when you'll need to read in one file, modify it, and then write a modified version of that file to a new file.

Given an input file, read the file and look for all occurrences of the word *utilize*. Replace each occurrence with *use*. Write the modified file to a new file.

Example Output

Given the input file of

```
One should never utilize the word "utilize" in
writing. Use "use" instead.
```

The program should generate

```
One should never use the word "use" in
writing. Use "use" instead.
```

Constraints

- Prompt for the name of the output file.
- Write the output to a new file.

Challenges

- Modify the program to track the number of replacements and report that to the screen when the program finishes.
- Create a configuration file that maps "bad" words to "good" words and use this file instead of a hard-coded value.
- Modify the program so it can handle a folder of files instead of a single file.

46 Word Frequency Finder

Knowing how often a word appears in a sentence or block of text is helpful for creating word clouds and other types of word analysis. And it's more useful when running it against lots of text.

Create a program that reads in a file and counts the frequency of words in the file. Then construct a histogram displaying the words and the frequency, and display the histogram to the screen.

Example Output

Given the text file words.txt with this content

```
badger badger badger badger mushroom mushroom
snake badger badger badger
```

the program would produce the following output:

```
badger:   *******
mushroom: **
snake:    *
```

Constraint

- Ensure that the most used word is at the top of the report and the least used words are at the bottom.

Challenges

- Use a graphical program and generate bar graphs.
- Test the performance of your calculation by providing a very large input file, such as Shakespeare's Macbeth.[1] Tweak your algorithm so that it performs the word counting as fast as possible.
- Write the program in another language and compare the processing times of the two implementations.

1. http://shakespeare.mit.edu/macbeth/full.html

What You Learned

Understanding how to read, write, and manipulate files from your programming language is a critical task, and now you've had a lot more practice. Of course, more practice helps you sharpen your skills, so consider revisiting the problems in Chapter 7, *Data Structures*, on page 63 and modifying them so you fetch the records from files instead of in memory.

But in our increasingly interconnected world, we might have to interact with data from other services located across the Internet. Let's look at how.

CHAPTER 9

Working with External Services

One of the most important skills a programmer can have is working with external services that provide data. Twitter, Flickr, Facebook, Google, and so many others expose their data through APIs, which is short for application programming interfaces.

Your application makes a request to the API, and the API responds with some data, which you process in your app. It may come in as XML data or JSON data, or sometimes you'll have to scrape results off the screen yourself.

Some APIs are freely available, but others require you to obtain access by registering as a developer. That adds some additional complexity to your programs because you'll need to come up with a way to securely store the keys. Professional software developers use version control software like Git, and if the keys are stored in the source code, it's easy to accidentally upload those keys to the version control system, or worse, to a site like GitHub where they become public. Yes, that's happened a few times.

If you're working with JavaScript in the browser, you can't just put that information in your JavaScript code, because everyone who runs your program will be able to view all of your code and steal your keys. So you'll want to consider using your own server-side proxy to handle the requests.

To complete the exercises in this chapter, you'll need to figure out how these third-party APIs work and how to integrate them into your programs. You'll need to read the documentation for each API to find out how to get the data and what format the data will be in, and then you'll have to look up how to request that data from your program and process those results.

47 Who's in Space?

Did you know you can find out exactly who's in space right now? The Open Notify API provides that information. Visit http://api.open-notify.org/astros.json to see not only how many people are currently in space but also their names and which spacecraft they're on.

Create a program that pulls in this data and displays the information from this API in a tabular format.

Example Output

```
There are 3 people in space right now:

Name                 | Craft
---------------------|------
Gennady Padalka      | ISS
Mikhail Kornienko    | ISS
Scott Kelly          | ISS
```

Constraint

- Read the data directly from the API and parse the results each time the program is run. Don't download the data as text and read it in.

Challenges

- Ensure that the width of the header is as long as the longest value in the column.
- Don't repeat the name of the craft—group all people by craft.
- Can you reliably sort the results alphabetically by last name? Be careful—some people have spaces in their name, like "Mary Sue Van Pelt."

48 Grabbing the Weather

Is it nice out today? Or should I grab my coat?

Using the OpenWeatherMap API at http://openweathermap.org/current, create a program that prompts for a city name and returns the current temperature for the city.

Example Output

```
Where are you? Chicago IL
Chicago weather:
65 degrees Fahrenheit
```

Constraint

- Keep the processing of the weather feed separate from the part of your program that displays the results.

Challenges

- The API gives the sunrise and sunset times, as well as the humidity and a description of the weather. Display that data in a meaningful way.
- The API gives the wind direction in degrees. Convert it to words such as "North," "West," "South," "Southwest," or even "South-southwest."
- Develop a scheme that lets the weather program tell you what kind of day it is. If it's 70 degrees and clear skies, say that it's a nice day out!
- Display the temperature in both Celsius and Fahrenheit.
- Based on the information, determine if the person needs a coat or an umbrella.

49 Flickr Photo Search

Some services provide search features and give you a lot of control over the results you get back. All you have to do is construct the right kind of request.

Create a program with a graphical interface that takes in a search string and displays photographs that match that search string. Use Flickr's public photo feed at https://www.flickr.com/services/feeds/docs/photos_public/ as your service.

Example Output

Your program should display the photographs like this:

Constraints

- Because this is a graphical program, you'll need to display the pictures from the API. If you're using JavaScript, do this with HTML and the DOM. Don't use jQuery or any external frameworks. If you're using Java, try building a desktop application with Swing or an Android application. If you're using a language without a rich GUI toolkit, create an HTML page and open it with the local browser.

Challenges

- If you're using JavaScript, implement this program using Angular, Ember, or React. Or do it once in each one if you're feeling up to the challenge.
- Use the Twitter API to find tweets associated with the search term and display them next to the picture.

50 Movie Recommendations

The data provided by external services can give you a jumping-off point to create your own application.

Write a program that displays information about a given movie. Prompt for a search query and display the title, year, rating, running time, and a synopsis, if one exists. Then, if the audience score is above 80%, recommend that the user watch this movie right now. If the score is below 50%, recommend that the user avoid the movie at all costs.

Example Output

```
Enter the name of a movie: Guardians of the Galaxy

Title: Guardians of the Galaxy
Year: 2014
Rating: PG-13
Running Time: 121 minutes

Description: From Marvel...

You should watch this movie right now!
```

Constraint

- Use the Rotten Tomatoes API at http://developer.rottentomatoes.com/ and obtain an API key.

Challenges

- Create a graphical version of the program. Display the movie poster image along with the rating information graphically.
- Investigate methods to cache the movie data you've collected so that you aren't constantly hitting the external API. Provide a method to expire the cache.

51 Pushing Notes to Firebase

Some external services allow you to update data, not just read it. Firebase[1] is a service that lets you create your own database so you can save data for web, mobile, and desktop applications. And you can use it with any programming language, thanks to its JSON-based API.

Create a simple command-line application that lets you save and show notes, using Firebase to save the notes. The application should support the following commands:

- mynotes new Learn how to invert binary trees should save the note.
- Use mynotes show to display all of the existing notes.

Example Output

```
$ mynotes new Learn how to invert binary trees
Your note was saved.

$ mynotes show
2050-12-31 - Learn how to invert binary trees
2050-12-30 - Notetaking on the command line is cool.
```

Constraints

- Create a configuration file that stores the API key.
- Use the REST documentation at https://www.firebase.com/docs/rest/ instead of a premade client library.

Challenges

- Create a more generalized application that lets you search for and view notes.
- Replace your implementation with one of the client libraries.
- Add the ability to tag notes.
- Revisit a few problems in Chapter 8, *Working with Files,* on page 75 and alter them to use Firebase.

1. https://www.firebase.com/

52 Creating Your Own Time Service

Consuming external services is one thing, but it's important to be able to create and consume your own service that others can use, so you can support other developers who want to use services you'll provide.

Create a simple web service that returns the current time as JSON data, such as: `{ "currentTime": "2050-01-24 15:06:26" }`.

Then create a client application that connects to the web service, parses the response, and displays the time.

Example Output

```
The current time is 15:06:26 UTC January 4 2050.
```

Constraints

- In your server application, be sure to set the content type to `application/json` when you send the response.
- Build the server app with as little code as possible.

Challenges

- Build a new server that displays a random quote. Store quotes in an array and pick one at random to display.
- Write a client-side component that displays the quotes in a different language than the one you used for the server.

What You Learned

Modern programs rely on third-party services, so it's good to know how to consume them, but you'll most likely find yourself using this pattern in your own work. It's common to have a native mobile application reading and writing data to a central back end written in a server-side language. Web applications routinely use client-side JavaScript to work with server-side JSON APIs. The experience you gain from these exercises is in great demand.

Now it's time to put together everything you've learned by tackling some more robust programs.

CHAPTER 10

Full Programs

If you've completed the other exercises, you're probably looking for a bigger challenge to flex your programming muscles. The exercises in this chapter will ask you to pull together everything you've learned. Some of these exercises will require you to step out of your comfort zone, and you may have to do a little research into your programming language's standard library to solve some of the problems here.

As you work on these exercises, think about the process we explored at the beginning of this book. Look at the problem statements and see how you can break down the problem into smaller units. Think of how you can write some test plans to ensure you know that your program will turn out right.

Also, see if you can identify patterns, or things you've done before in previous programs. It's common to use the same approach to solve different problems.

53 Todo List

Let's start with the good-old trusty todo list, the "Hello, World" of full programs. You're going to write a command-line todo list program that meets the following specifications:

- Prompt the user to enter a chore or task. Store the task in a permanent location so that the task persists when the program is restarted.
- Allow the user to enter as many tasks as desired but stop entering tasks by entering a blank task. *Do not store the blank task.*
- Display all the tasks.
- Allow the user to remove a task, to signify it's been completed.

Constraints

- Store the data in an external data source.
- If you're using a server-side language, consider persisting the data to Redis.
- Consider persisting the database to a third-party service like Parse or Firebase.

Challenges

- Implement this in a web browser using only front-end technologies. Investigate using IndexedDB to save the items.
- Implement the front end as an Android or iPhone app, but connect that front end to your own back end that you write using a server-side language. Create your own API for retrieving the list, creating a new item, and marking an item as complete.

54 URL Shortener

Write a web application that allows users to take a long URL and convert it to a shortened URL similar to `https://goo.gl/`.

- The program should have a form that accepts the long URL.
- The program should generate a short local URL like `/abc1234` and store the short URL and the long URL together in a persistent data store.
- The program should redirect visitors to the long URL when the short URL is visited.
- The program should track the number of times the short URL is visited.
- The program should have a statistics page for the short URL, such as `/abc1234/stats`. Visiting this URL should show the short URL, the long URL, and the number of times the short URL was accessed.

Constraints

- This app must use a persistent data store that others can use. That means a local, in-memory system isn't appropriate.
- Don't allow an invalid URL to be entered into the form.

Challenges

- Detect duplicate URLs. Don't create a new short URL if one already exists.
- Use Redis as your data store.
- Use RavenDB as your data store.
- Record the date and time each short URL was accessed, and use a graphing library to graph the requests.

55 Text Sharing

Create a web application that lets users share a snippet of text, similar to http://pastie.org. The program you write should follow these specifications:

- The user should enter the text into a text area and save the text.
- The text should be stored in a data store.
- The program should generate a URL that can be used to retrieve the saved text.
- When a user follows that URL, the text should be displayed, along with an invitation to edit the text.
- When a user clicks the Edit button, the text should be copied and placed in the same interface used to create new text snippets.

Constraint

- Use something other than a primary key for the URL, such as a slug that you generate. Investigate SHA or MD5 hashing.

Challenges

- Modify the program so that each paste supports Markdown formatting.
- Modify the program so that the `edit` functionality edits the existing node and keeps versions of previous notes.
- Implement an API and make a command-line, native, or mobile application that can add new text snippets or view snippets.

56 Tracking Inventory

Write a program that tracks your personal inventory. The program should allow you to enter an item, a serial number, and estimated value. The program should then be able to print out a tabular report in both HTML and CSV formats that looks like this:

Name	Serial Number	Value
Xbox One	AXB124AXY	$399.00
Samsung TV	S40AZBDE4	$599.99

Constraints

- Store the data in a persistent local data file in JSON, XML, or YAML format.
- Require numeric data for the value of each item.

Challenges

- Alter the program so that it can store photos. If you're creating this application for a mobile device, allow the user to take a picture with the camera.
- Allow the items to be searchable.

57 Trivia App

Create a multiple-choice trivia application.

- Read questions, answers, and distractors (wrong answers) from a file.
- When a player starts a game
  - Choose questions at random.
  - Display the answer and distractors in a random order.
  - Track the number of correct answers.
  - End the game when the player selects a wrong answer.

Constraint

- Write this file using a file database or local data file rather than a key-value store or a relational database.

Challenges

- Add a difficulty field for the questions, and present increasingly difficult questions as the game progresses.
- Expand the program by adding a mode that allows a parent or teacher to add, edit, or remove questions and answers.

Where to Go Next

With these programs, you hopefully have some mastery over the programming language you chose to use and you can start thinking about some of your own problems you'd like to solve. One of the best ways to dig deep into a language or a framework is to use it to scratch your own itch. Think about the issues in your life that you'd like to tackle. Or try to rewrite an existing application. Write your own calorie-counting app, pomodoro timer, or grocery list app.

Learn the other important tools of the software development trade. Explore test-driven development and work with the tools available in your language to write unit and acceptance tests. Then investigate version control with Git and post your code to GitHub[1] so others can see it. Or apply your new skills toward contributing to an open-source project. It's a great way to learn from others and advance your career.

And when it comes time to learn your next language, pick up this book again and start at the beginning, but incorporate new ways of thinking to solve these familiar problems. Happy coding!

1. http://github.com

The Joy of Mazes and Math

Rediscover the joy and fascinating weirdness of mazes and pure mathematics.

Mazes for Programmers

A book on mazes? Seriously?

Yes!

Not because you spend your day creating mazes, or because you particularly like solving mazes.

But because it's fun. Remember when programming used to be fun? This book takes you back to those days when you were starting to program, and you wanted to make your code do things, draw things, and solve puzzles. It's fun because it lets you explore and grow your code, and reminds you how it feels to just think.

Sometimes it feels like you live your life in a maze of twisty little passages, all alike. Now you can code your way out.

Jamis Buck
(286 pages) ISBN: 9781680500554. $38
https://pragprog.com/book/jbmaze

Good Math

Mathematics is beautiful—and it can be fun and exciting as well as practical. *Good Math* is your guide to some of the most intriguing topics from two thousand years of mathematics: from Egyptian fractions to Turing machines; from the real meaning of numbers to proof trees, group symmetry, and mechanical computation. If you've ever wondered what lay beyond the proofs you struggled to complete in high school geometry, or what limits the capabilities of the computer on your desk, this is the book for you.

Mark C. Chu-Carroll
(282 pages) ISBN: 9781937785338. $34
https://pragprog.com/book/mcmath

Seven in Seven

You need to learn at least one new language every year. Here are fourteen excellent suggestions to get started.

Seven Languages in Seven Weeks

You should learn a programming language every year, as recommended by *The Pragmatic Programmer*. But if one per year is good, how about *Seven Languages in Seven Weeks*? In this book you'll get a hands-on tour of Clojure, Haskell, Io, Prolog, Scala, Erlang, and Ruby. Whether or not your favorite language is on that list, you'll broaden your perspective of programming by examining these languages side-by-side. You'll learn something new from each, and best of all, you'll learn how to learn a language quickly.

Bruce A. Tate
(330 pages) ISBN: 9781934356593. $34.95
https://pragprog.com/book/btlang

Seven More Languages in Seven Weeks

Great programmers aren't born—they're made. The industry is moving from object-oriented languages to functional languages, and you need to commit to radical improvement. New programming languages arm you with the tools and idioms you need to refine your craft. While other language primers take you through basic installation and "Hello, World," we aim higher. Each language in *Seven More Languages in Seven Weeks* will take you on a step-by-step journey through the most important paradigms of our time. You'll learn seven exciting languages: Lua, Factor, Elixir, Elm, Julia, MiniKanren, and Idris.

Bruce Tate, Fred Daoud, Jack Moffitt, Ian Dees
(320 pages) ISBN: 9781941222157. $38
https://pragprog.com/book/7lang

More Seven in Seven

From Web Frameworks to Concurrency Models, see what the rest of the world is doing with this introduction to seven different approaches.

Seven Web Frameworks in Seven Weeks

Whether you need a new tool or just inspiration, *Seven Web Frameworks in Seven Weeks* explores modern options, giving you a taste of each with ideas that will help you create better apps. You'll see frameworks that leverage modern programming languages, employ unique architectures, live client-side instead of server-side, or embrace type systems. You'll see everything from familiar Ruby and JavaScript to the more exotic Erlang, Haskell, and Clojure.

Jack Moffitt, Fred Daoud
(302 pages) ISBN: 9781937785635. $38
https://pragprog.com/book/7web

Seven Concurrency Models in Seven Weeks

Your software needs to leverage multiple cores, handle thousands of users and terabytes of data, and continue working in the face of both hardware and software failure. Concurrency and parallelism are the keys, and *Seven Concurrency Models in Seven Weeks* equips you for this new world. See how emerging technologies such as actors and functional programming address issues with traditional threads and locks development. Learn how to exploit the parallelism in your computer's GPU and leverage clusters of machines with MapReduce and Stream Processing. And do it all with the confidence that comes from using tools that help you write crystal clear, high-quality code.

Paul Butcher
(296 pages) ISBN: 9781937785659. $38
https://pragprog.com/book/pb7con

The Pragmatic Bookshelf

The Pragmatic Bookshelf features books written by developers for developers. The titles continue the well-known Pragmatic Programmer style and continue to garner awards and rave reviews. As development gets more and more difficult, the Pragmatic Programmers will be there with more titles and products to help you stay on top of your game.

Visit Us Online

This Book's Home Page
https://pragprog.com/book/bhwb
Source code from this book, errata, and other resources. Come give us feedback, too!

Register for Updates
https://pragprog.com/updates
Be notified when updates and new books become available.

Join the Community
https://pragprog.com/community
Read our weblogs, join our online discussions, participate in our mailing list, interact with our wiki, and benefit from the experience of other Pragmatic Programmers.

New and Noteworthy
https://pragprog.com/news
Check out the latest pragmatic developments, new titles and other offerings.

Save on the eBook

Save on the eBook versions of this title. Owning the paper version of this book entitles you to purchase the electronic versions at a terrific discount.

PDFs are great for carrying around on your laptop—they are hyperlinked, have color, and are fully searchable. Most titles are also available for the iPhone and iPod touch, Amazon Kindle, and other popular e-book readers.

Buy now at *https://pragprog.com/coupon*

Contact Us

Online Orders:	*https://pragprog.com/catalog*
Customer Service:	*support@pragprog.com*
International Rights:	*translations@pragprog.com*
Academic Use:	*academic@pragprog.com*
Write for Us:	*http://write-for-us.pragprog.com*
Or Call:	+1 800-699-7764

Printed in the USA
CPSIA information can be obtained
at www.ICGtesting.com
JSHW010854191024
72015JS00018B/630

9 781680 501223